THE WONDERFUL WORLD OF WORDS

7

The Queen's Best Friend

Dr Lubna Alsagoff

PhD (Stanford)

mc Marshall Cavendish
Children

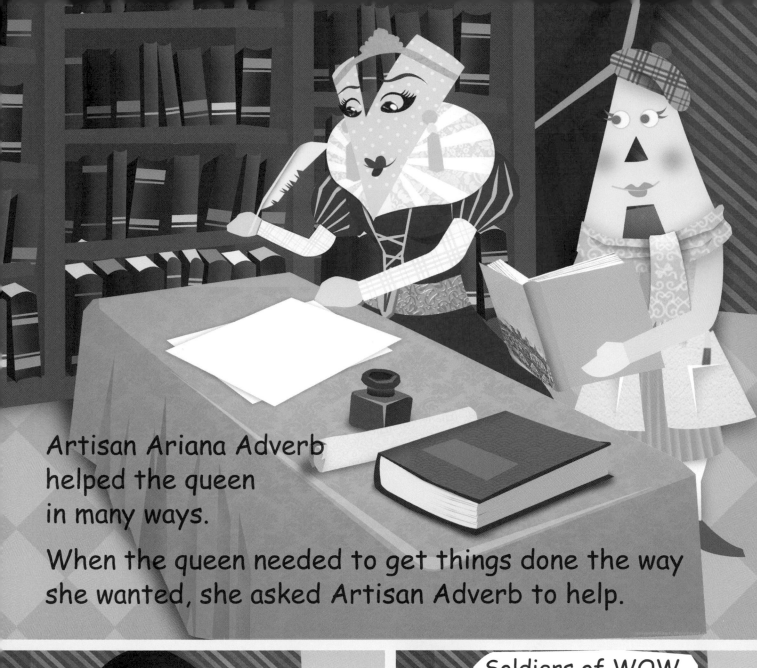

Artisan Ariana Adverb helped the queen in many ways.

When the queen needed to get things done the way she wanted, she asked Artisan Adverb to help.

Soldiers of WOW, run!

Soldiers of WOW, run quickly!

2

3

Queen Verb and Artisan Adverb
were best friends.

Adverbs go together with verbs.
Adverbs tell us more about verbs.

King Noun also had a good friend,
Admiral Adjective.

Adjectives go together with nouns.
Adjectives tell us more about nouns.

Admiral Adjective wrote a beautiful song.

Artisan Adverb sang it beautifully.

9

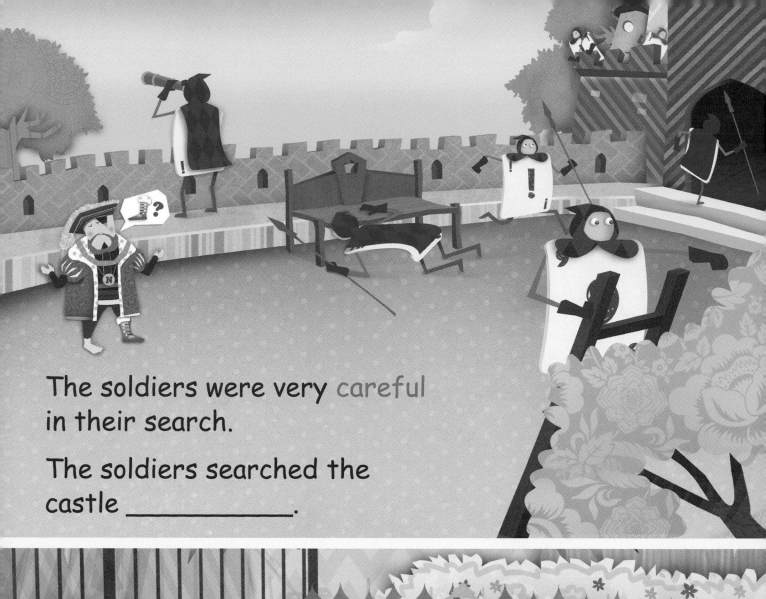

The soldiers were very careful in their search.

The soldiers searched the castle _____.

The queen thought Artisan Adverb's paintings were wonderful.

The queen thought Artisan Adverb painted _____.

The admiral's ship was _____.

The admiral's ship sailed swiftly.

Prince Pronoun gave an eloquent speech about WOW.

Prince Pronoun spoke _____ about WOW.

 Adjective

 Noun

long •

• grass

sharp •

• cat

green •

• beard

black •

• knife

12

 **Verb**

 **Adverb**

sing

•   •   gracefully

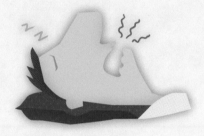
snore

•   •   slowly

dance

•   •   loudly

crawl

•   •   beautifully

Fill in the right adjective or adverb.
Can you say whether the word you
used is an adjective or adverb?
Which word does it describe?

The king loved walking in the
<u>beautiful</u> gardens of WOW.
<u>Beautiful</u> is an <u>adjective</u> because
it describes the <u>noun gardens</u>.

Princess Preposition rowed
_____ across the lake.
_____ is an _____ because
it describes the _____ _____ .

After his meal, Cappy, the
_____ caterpillar, fell fast asleep.
_____ is an _____ because
it describes the _____ _____ .

The fox ran _____ to her den
to make sure her children were safe.
_____ is an _____ because
it describes the _____ _____ .

The _____ soldiers needed to sit and rest after their exercise. _____ is an _____ because it describes the _____ _____ .

The builders worked _____ to repair the broken shelter. _____ is an _____ because it describes the _____ _____ .

The children were so _____ playing with each other. _____ is an _____ because it describes the _____ _____ .

Prince Pronoun was a very _____ speaker. _____ is an _____ because it describes the _____ _____ .

The dancer stood on her toes and twirled so _____. _____ is an _____ because it describes the _____ _____ .

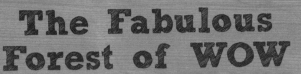

The Fabulous Forest of WOW

Owl continued to read the WOW Grammar Book carefully to learn as much as he could.

He taught Rabbit and Squirrel so that they could work with him to help the animals of the forest.

Did you know that words are not all the same?

Yes, words are different because they have different meanings.

That's right! **Big** is the opposite of **small**.

small

big

The word **clock** means a different thing from the word **watch**. So you know that you hang clocks on the wall, but you wear watches!

Yes, that is true. But words are also different in the way they are used in a sentence.

So even though two words mean the same thing, they are sometimes used differently.

beautiful   beautifully

The word **beautiful** and **beautifully** mean the same thing — that someone or something looks very nice.

beautiful   beautifully

Oh yes, they look alike, but **beautifully** looks a little different — it has a word ending **ly**.

beautiful song | sing beautifully
beautiful picture | paint beautifully

But they are used in different ways. **Beautiful** goes with words like **song** and **picture**. **Beautifully** goes with words like **sing** and **paint**.

beautiful sing ✗ | song beautifully ✗
beautiful paint ✗ | picture beautifully ✗

You cannot switch the words around!

Let's write down the words that have this pattern.

loud   `l` `o` `u` `d` `l` `y`

sad   `s` `a` `d` ☐ ☐

sweet   `s` `w` `e` `e` `t` ☐ ☐

nice   ☐ ☐ ☐ ☐ ☐ ☐

quick   ☐ ☐ ☐ ☐ ☐ ☐ ☐

quiet   ☐ ☐ ☐ ☐ ☐ ☐ ☐

careful   ☐ ☐ ☐ ☐ ☐ ☐ ☐ ☐ ☐

Words can be grouped together.

slow
wonderful
careless
beautiful
happy
quick

slowly
quickly
beautifully
happily
wonderfully
carelessly

The green cloud contains words that are called _____ .

These words describe _____ .

The blue cloud contains words that are called _____ .

These words describe _____ .

Dear Parents,

In this issue, children should notice and learn:

- Adverbs describe or tell you more about verbs.

- This is similar to how adjectives describe nouns.

- They should notice that many adverbs look like adjectives, except that they have an *ly* ending. Though not all adverbs have the ending, we begin by teaching children how to notice this difference in the more common adverbs.

Page	Possible Answers
4–5	You can use many different adverbs with the verbs. Here are some suggestions: march quickly | happily | boldly tiptoe carefully | quietly | silently laugh loudly | softly | heartily rest quietly | silently
10–11	carefully wonderfully swift eloquently
14–15	There are many possible ways to fill in the blanks. Here are some suggestions: **carefully** — carefully is an adverb because it describes the verb row. **hungry** — hungry is an adjective because it describes the noun caterpillar. **quickly** — quickly is an adverb because it describes the verb run. **tired** — tired is an adjective because it describes the noun soldiers. **together** — together is an adverb because it describes the verb work. **happy** — happy is an adjective because it describes the noun children. **eloquent** — eloquent is an adjective because it describes the noun speaker. **gracefully** — gracefully is an adverb because it describes the verb twirl.
23	adverbs | verbs adjectives | nouns

24